W9-BAE-428

# *Fjords of Blue Ice*

## *Alaska's Endicott & Tracy Arm*

*Featuring Dawes and Sawyer Glaciers*

Publisher: Mark Kelley
Photographer: Mark Kelley
Author: Nick Jans
Designers: Matt Knutson, Laura Lucas
Digital Imaging Specialist: Terra Dawn Parker
Project Manager: Malou Peabody
Proofreader: Tina Brown, Leandra Lewis

Printed in Canada by Friesens Corporation
A FSC® certified printer, a proud member of the Green Press Initiative

Mailing Address: Mark Kelley / PO Box 32077 / Juneau, AK 99803 / USA
Business Phone: (907) 586-1993 or Toll Free: (888) 933-1993
FAX Number: (907) 586-1201
Email: photos@markkelley.com
Website: markkelley.com

First Printing: 2016
ISBN: 9781880865354

COVER: A blue iceberg that originated from the Dawes Glacier in the distance is carried away by tidal forces.
BACK COVER: A cruise ship travels toward South Sawyer Glacier in Tracy Arm.
HALF-TITLE PAGE: The day boat, Adventure Bound, passes in front of South Sawyer Glacier.
TITLE-PAGE: The Spirit of Columbia approaches icebergs in Tracy Arm.

# Fjords of Blue Ice

## Alaska's Endicott & Tracy Arm

photos by **MARK KELLEY**
written by **NICK JANS**

Harbor seals rest on ice.

*Our vessel glides inland,* away from the sweep of ocean waves, threading between icebergs that shimmer blue and white. On either side of the narrowing passage, walls of sheer granite tower skyward, cut by waterfalls and cascades. Through binoculars, a distant speck above becomes a mountain goat; farther along, seals sunning on a raft of ice regard us with dark, liquid eyes. Carved glacial domes and ragged nunataks a mile above us reflect on the water's surface, and below our hull, the cold, green depths of the fjord whisper a tidal pulse old as time.

by NICK JANS

Passengers on board a day tour boat cruise through icebergs on the way to Sawyer Glacier, often referred to as North Sawyer Glacier.

Mountain goat.

## *Tracy Arm—Fords Terror Wilderness*

includes one of the most spectacular glacial fjord systems in both Alaska and the world. Glacier Bay National Park, roughly 125 miles to the northwest, is far better known, and Misty Fjords, near Ketchikan, is duly celebrated. But Tracy Arm, 32 miles long and averaging a mile wide, surrounded by steep mountain walls rising up to 7,000 feet from sea level, surrenders nothing in grandeur or vertical scale to any of these treasures. In fact, it gains its visual power from the fact that so much is crammed into such a compact space. Its companion to the south, 35-mile long Endicott Arm, features the dramatic, current-ripped narrows of Fords Terror and a breathtaking vista at the face of Dawes Glacier. This spectacular wilderness preserve reminds us, residents and travelers alike, why we came to Alaska.

RIGHT: The Coast Mountains separate Alaska from Canada, and serve as a backdrop for the Sawyer Glacier (sometimes referred to as North Sawyer Glacier).

The two peaks between the Sawyer and South Sawyer Glaciers rise more than 7,000 feet from the aqua blue waters of Tracy Arm.

## *"A wild unfinished Yosemite"*

Famed naturalist John Muir thought enough of Tracy Arm to call it, after two visits in the late 19th century, "a wild unfinished Yosemite," and to proclaim that "no ice work I have ever seen surpasses this, either in the magnitude of the features or effectiveness of composition." Quite an accolade from a man who explored some of the roughest and wildest terrain in the Pacific Northwest, including Glacier Bay. Considering that the Grand Canyon, at its deepest point 6,000 feet, has 1,000 feet less vertical relief, it's hardly an overstatement.

Waterfalls cascade down thousands of feet of barren rock walls revealed by the glacier's retreat.

## SOUTHEAST ALASKA
Dayboat route from Juneau to Tracy Arm

Juneau

*Taku Inlet*

Grand
I.

*Taku Harbor*

*Port Snettisham*

ADMIRALTY
I.

TRACY ARM-
FORDS TERROR
WILDERNESS

*Stephens Passage*

ALASKA

Map area

KUPREANOF
I.

Petersburg

Three narrow, mountain-rimmed fjords – Tracy, Endicott, and Fords Terror –make up the Tracy Arm-Fords Terror Wilderness, about 45 miles southeast of Juneau. While relatively petite by Alaska standards, this preserve, overseen by the U.S. Forest Service, is nonetheless immense. Extending eastward to the Canadian border, it enfolds 653,179 acres of the ragged, soaring Coast Mountains, those three dramatic fjords and their meeting place at Holkham Bay, plus three tidewater glaciers (Sawyer, South Sawyer and Dawes) – not to mention a sizeable hunk of the Stikine Icefield, which feeds those three, as well as dozens of smaller mountain glaciers. This is a near-vertical landscape of ice, water and stone, where vegetation struggles for footholds and sheer cliffs of 500 to 1,000 feet are commonplace. Yet, due to coastal mists and steady year-round precipitation (this is, after all, a temperate rainforest), bands of verdant greenery add contrast to the dominating starkness. Due to the rugged nature of the terrain, the only practical way to explore the area is via the deep, saltwater passages carved into this wilderness by hands of ice. And, while the longer Endicott and its offshoot, Fords Terror, present their own spectacular beauty (the latter, as its dramatic name suggests, is guarded at a narrow passage by roiling tidal currents), Tracy Arm is widely regarded as the most visually dramatic of the three fjords.

ABOVE: Aerial view of South Sawyer
Glacier and Sawyer Island.

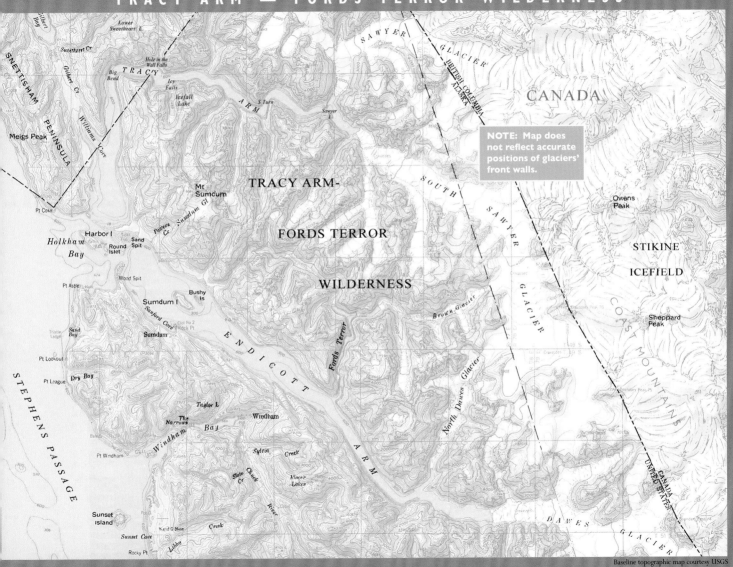

NOTE: Map does not reflect accurate positions of glaciers' front walls.

Visitors on the *Adventure Bound* survey the ice-choked water in front of Sawyer Glacier.

*The first human inhabitants* of the area – the Tlingit Indians and their ancestors – left few signs of their presence inside Tracy Arm proper, where the near-vertical landscape discouraged settlements. No doubt the abundance of seals attracted hunters. Muir noted a Tlingit fort on Round Island at the mouth of Holkham Bay and a village at Powers Creek in Endicott Arm. However, these settlements were abandoned in the 1900's. Gold miners came and went, as well as fox farmers who used the islands in Holkham and Endicott Arm as pens. But these,

too, dwindled. Today, there are no permanent residents inside Holkham Bay proper, although U.S. Forest Service rangers patrol the area by kayak six months a year, monitoring resource use and assisting researchers. The single person most familiar with Tracy Arm is tour boat operator Steve Weber, captain of the Adventure Bound. He's toured the waters of Tracy Arm for over thirty seasons. "It's marvelous every day," he says. "Constantly changing. You don't get into a routine, ever. You just take the day as it comes, and it's always rewarding."

Icebergs that calve off the face of South Sawyer Glacier range in color from white to deep glacier blue.

## *A monument to the power of ice*

Tracy Arm-Fords Terror Wilderness stands, above all, as a monument to the power of ice. The landscape was carved by its unimaginable force, a dynamic process that continues to this day. Picture a solid block of stone (predominately erosion-resistant granite, marble and schist, with deposits of softer slate, green schist and limestone) 35 miles long and 5 wide – billions of cubic tons, up-thrust into jagged, soaring peaks. This was the raw material from which this fjord and its setting were cut by a wall of ice more than a mile thick, and by the grinding power of the rock it moved. During the height of the Pleistocene Age, the current glacial epoch, this ice monster shifted relentlessly across the land. It lumbered seaward, pulled by the force of gravity, gouging and shaping as it went, the weight so immense that it bowed the underlying bedrock. When it met the ocean, its front face, undercut as it was shoved forward, calved in immense blue shards.

### TIP OF THE ICEBERG

About 80 to 90 percent of an iceberg remains below the surface of the water. Glacier ice is less dense than the surrounding seawater, and therefore floats with its bulk largely hidden. This explains the expression, "tip of the iceberg."

The grandeur of South Sawyer Glacier dwarfs one of the many tour vessels that visit Tracy Arm.

A 32-foot boat passes by the glacier-carved, vertical cliffs of Tracy Arm.

## *...walls more than 8,000 feet high*

So much of the world's water was tied up in ice that the ocean's level was far lower than it is today. The floor of Tracy Arm, at its deepest spot more than 1,200 feet below sea level, was once the bottom of a U-shaped valley with walls more than 8,000 feet high. Only the tips of the tallest surrounding peaks, known as nunataks, escaped the glacial scouring. Here a few plants and animals found refuge from the pouring river of ice, and some survived to later repopulate the land as the flood receded. Today these nunataks are visible as ragged sentinels, rising over domes that, like the walls below them, bear the horizontal striations of their sculptor's massive hand.

At its peak, the ice wall extended to the mouth of Holkham Bay, the entry point to the Tracy Arm-Fords Terror Wilderness. Here lies a terminal moraine, – a huge, oblong mound of rocky rubble pushed there by the glacier itself – that today forms a reef through which the relentless tides have carved narrow passages into Tracy and Edicott Arms.

RIGHT: Horizontal striations, evidence of the glacier's advance and retreat, scar the rock walls.

## ...clogged with drifting, grinding ice

Since roughly 12,000 years ago, the Stikine Icefield has been generally receding – though with numerous surges forward. The most recent advance began in the 13th century and ended just over 150 years ago. The ice front has been in constant flux. In 1794, a party from British explorer George Vancouver's expedition briefly entered Holkham Bay and reported "much floating ice," but little else. We can't say where the glacial front lay, aside from the obvious fact it was farther in. A century later, John Muir bore due north from the mouth of Holkham and entered Tracy Arm itself. His report includes only one glacier, suggesting that Sawyer (sometimes referred to as North Sawyer) and South Sawyer Glaciers, currently separated by about six water miles, were connected at the time much farther down the fjord. Since then, the retreat shows no sign of abating. While glaciers always flow downslope, both Sawyers and Endicott Arm's Dawes Glacier are receding, meaning, the rate of calving and melting exceeds their advance. The most active of the three is South Sawyer – which in 2004 and 2016

The 120-person catamaran glides by the South Sawyer Glacier face.

calved so profusely that the entire upper Arm clogged with drifting, grinding ice. Meanwhile, the Sawyer Glacier retreated almost 1 3/4 miles (2.8 km.) between 1990 and 2013. The western feeder of Sawyer has narrowed from a bit more than 3000 feet in 1990 to about 1500 feet in 2013. As a matter of fact, in a very short time the western and eastern feeders of the Sawyer Glacier will separate. Note that the recession in Tracy Arm-Ford Terror has been so rapid that the most up-to-date maps and charts don't reflect the position of either glacier's front wall.

### STIKINE ICEFIELD

More than 500 square miles in size, the Stikine Icefield is the birthplace of three tidewater glaciers: the Sawyer, South Sawyer, and Dawes Glaciers. Icefields form high in the mountains wherever annual snowfall exceeds annual snow melt.

Think of an icefield as a lake of ice from which glaciers flow like rivers. In the Stikine Icefield, over 100 feet of snow falls every year. The weight of all this new snow pressurizes the old snow layers underneath, and over time snow crystals will metamorphose into ice crystals. With the relatively mild temperatures of Southeast Alaska, snow in the Stikine Icefield can turn into glacier ice in just four to six years. As glacier ice continues to form over time, the ice in the icefield will spill over into its glaciers, where gravity takes hold. These frozen rivers of ice, snow, and rock flow downslope, carving the landscape.

LEFT: An iceberg is stuck in a submerged bar that was created by the last terminal moraine of the Sawyer Glaciers in Holkham Bay, at the entrance to both Tracy and Endicott Arm.

## RETREAT / RECEDING

Despite a constant flow downhill, the Sawyer, South Sawyer, and Dawes Glaciers are receding, or retreating. Simply put, these glaciers are losing ice faster than they can transport it. Over the eons, glaciers have advanced and retreated according to the cycles of climatic warming and cooling. The current global warming trend has about 95 percent of the world's glaciers retreating.

Until 2004, the three tidewater glaciers in Tracy Arm-Fords Terror Wilderness were in a stable, somewhat predictable retreat. That summer both Sawyers experienced a step-change retreat (a relative stable period in a glacier's life mixed with sudden rapid retreats) and the 20-mile long South Sawyer Glacier lost over half a mile. It was as if the glacier started galloping backwards. Surface water temperatures in the fjord that summer measured 1.5 degrees warmer than usual. In 2010 Sawyer Glacier experienced a separate step-change retreat.

LEFT: Iceberg soup chokes the passageway to the South Sawyer Glacier.

A private boat approaches the
Hole in the Wall Waterfall.

The journey up Tracy Arm is longer than 32 miles; it's a passage back into time, to a world our Pleistocene ancestors must have known intimately. In a matter of miles, we pass through centuries of change, traced by the succession of vegetation patterns. Near the Arm's mouth, the world is comparatively soft and green, with broad patches of spruce and western hemlock. As we travel inland 10 miles, past the "big bend" – a dramatic 90-degree turn in the fjord's course from north to east – these evergreens diminish in frequency and size and gradually give way to pioneering bands of birch, willow and alder. In other places, early anchoring species such as lichens, fireweed and sedges cling to toeholds in the rock. As we near the Arm's head, barren, striated granite walls predominate, and we end our journey at shifting walls of ice: Sawyer and South Sawyer glaciers. Each is bordered by newly exposed rock that lay under a cold, shifting mantle of ice for untold centuries. In this succession, there are no precise demarcations; the shifts are more patchwork than regular, based on local conditions including exposure, steepness, and available soil. Given time, the power of growing roots, running water, and the cycle of freezing and thawing will eventually break down even dominant granite into soil, and the earth will blaze green. Or perhaps the tide of ice will turn and the glaciers will surge anew over the land, erasing all in their path as they have before. The only constant in Tracy Arm is change.

A passenger on board the motor vessel *Delphinus* tests out her rain jacket under the waterfalls at the entrance to Fords Terror in Endicott Arm.

The Sawyer Glacier, sometimes
referred to as North Sawyer Glacier.

## The twin Sawyers

Though John Muir noted one continuous glacier in his 1880 visit to Tracy Arm, a photo taken in 1900 for the Territorial Boundary Commission shows two separate glaciers, which were named accordingly: the Sawyer to the north, and South Sawyer, stretching toward the head of Tracy Arm. Given that Muir's observations were usually spot on, apparently the ice front had retreated far enough in just two decades to force that dramatic split—one that continues to widen to this day. Both glaciers flow from the same source—the vast Stikine Icefield, straddling the border of British Columbia and Alaska. Though diminished, the twin Sawyers are still imposing. The craggy, blue-white face of each rises over 200 feet above the water's surface, and extends hundreds of feet below the water level. Continually undercut by tidal flow, the downhill-grinding ice fronts shatter in thunderous geysers; calving displays range from paltry car-sized chunks to bergs weighing a hundred ton or more. Truly, these are worlds in collision, cast on a scale that would still awe Muir.

South Sawyer Glacier

Sumdum Glacier is a hanging glacier sitting at the entrance of Holkham Bay.

## A perfect finish . . .

In horse-racing terms, Endicott Arm is a sleeper—a bit deceiving at the start, with few hints of how well it will end. A third longer than Tracy Arm, with lower walls over most of its course, and averaging a mile wider, Endicott takes its time. Of course, beauty is a relative term. In a land where 2,000-foot, waterfall-spangled cliffs are commonplace, it's easy to overlook the spectacular. Just past the current-ripped terminal moraine at its entrance in Holkham Bay, Sumdum Glacier looms—a picture-perfect example of a hanging glacier, one that no longer reaches tidewater. Named after the Tlingit tribe that once made this area their home (literally, Dungeness Crab Town Tribe), Sumdum Glacier remains, a fitting emblem of a proud tradition, and another time. The Sumdum people apparently relocated after gold strikes

RIGHT: Rafters and a lone kayaker watch in amazement as ice calves of the front of Dawes Glacier at the end of Endicott Arm.

At the top of Endicott Arm, a cruise ship approaches the face of Dawes Glacier.

were made at Powers Creek in 1869, one of the first gold discoveries in the Alaska territory. A bustling mining town named Sumdum sprung up in the shadow of the glacier, complete with its own brewery, a post office, and a 3,000-foot mining tram. At its peak more than a century ago, the Sumdum Chief Mine produced more than 20,000 ounces of gold yearly. Today, few traces remain of this historic settlement, or of the people who came before.

Endicott Arm continues its 35-mile path, angling inland to the southeast, down a glacier-carved valley sunken millennia ago by rising sea levels. Stands of western hemlock, Sitka spruce, willow, and alder seek life in a world of stone, roots clinging to near-vertical crevices and geologic faults. Despite its austerity, the land is alive. Small mammals and a myriad of birds make their homes here. Black bears and mountain goats forage, sometimes down to the tideline. Harbor seals bask on icebergs and granite ledges. Somehow, life finds a way.

As we journey inland, chunks of glacial ice become more frequent. The bergs become larger, and some are still tinted with the haunting blue prevalent of highly compressed glacier ice. The 25-mile-long Dawes heaves into view, the terrain becomes more barren, the walls steeper and higher. As in Tracy Arm, the granite domes that line the fjord are reminiscent of those

in Yosemite, but cast on a grander scale.

We float on the restless tides at the foot of Dawes Glacier, and we know why we came. The glacier's jumbled, half-mile-long face rumbles and calves, shedding house-sized chunks of blue and white ice in thunderous geysers. Terns and gulls wheel; harbor seals dive among drifting bergs. On either side of the glacier, smaller u-shaped valleys rise toward hanging glaciers—classic fjord formations as dramatic as any on the planet. And rising above the glacier, a series of unnamed peaks thrust skyward, the tallest reaching over 7,000 feet. Endicott's finish is beyond breathtaking and spectacular. It's perfect.

Classic u-shaped, glacier carved valleys sit on both sides of Dawes Glacier.

## What's in a name?

Four-mile-long Fords Terror, by far the smallest of the three fjords, is also the least visited—for good reason. A mile in, voyagers are met by an alarming spectacle: a tight, curving channel swept by currents so intense that, as low tide approaches, it becomes a whitewater rapid—one that reverses direction when the tide turns and begins rushing back in. Beyond that fierce passage, scarcely 200 yards long, a green whirlpool boils along the base of a jutting cliff. According to local lore, a crew member of an 1899 expedition named Ford set out from Endicott Arm, alone in a wooden rowboat, intent on exploring the inlet. Apparently he hit that bottleneck sometime around slack tide, when the current slows, and passed through without incident. Continuing onward, he spent the day roaming the sheltered fjord, and no doubt marveled at the sculpted granite faces towering above him. Maybe he even fantasized

The motor vessel, *Delphinus*, cruises through the entrance to Fords Terror at high tide. At low tide the entrance is marked by standing waves.

A US Forest Service Ranger patrols the wilderness waters by a set of waterfalls just outside the entrance to Fords Terror.

about having some feature of the place named in his honor. On his outward run, the intrepid Ford was horrified to find his way out blocked by an inrushing maelstrom that hadn't existed just hours before. Panicked, he struggled to row against the overpowering 8-to-12-knot current and was time and again buffeted and swept back. The whirlpool must have spun his little craft like a windblown leaf. Ford was trapped alone for six harrowing hours until the current slackened; the standing waves lay down, and he rowed out to his ship as easily as he'd come in. If he had wished to leave his name on the landscape, he succeeded—though probably not in the way he'd imagined.

In a modern, smaller touring vessel at the hands of a knowledgeable skipper, the passage into this little gem of a fjord qualifies as thrilling, but hardly a white-knuckle experience. The near-vertical scenery that lies beyond that gateway is both grand and intimate, due to the narrow span of the fjord walls. Each of the two short branches features a procession of exquisite glacier-sculpted, curving granite formations accented by dramatic waterfalls and unique tidal meadows. Mile-high and taller peaks rising from tidewater are commonplace. Mountain goats are often visible on high slopes, and Fords Terror offers the sharp-eyed viewer the best opportunity in the Wilderness to see a bear grazing along the shore.

A motor boat from a small cruise ship brings back its passengers after exploring the upper reaches of Fords Terror.

Waterfall inside Fords Terror.

This granite dome located inside Fords Terror and the many other granite domes strung along the Arms' waterways reminds one of the glacier carved features of Yosemite National Park in California.

Cruise ship passengers enjoy a side trip in an inflatable boat.

## The pure spectacle of ice

Given the origins of Tracy Arm-Fords Terror Wilderness, it's only fitting that so many travelers are lured by the pure spectacle of ice. The dramatic, crevasse-riddled faces of Sawyer Glacier and that of its larger sister, South Sawyer, reign over the upper Arm, mysterious and ever-changing, sometimes shearing off in thunderous displays. Sawyer is roughly a quarter-mile across and eight miles long; South Sawyer is three times longer and half again as wide. Both average 200 feet in height where they meet tidewater, though the ice face continues far below the waterline – 300 additional feet at Sawyer, and an incredible 900 feet at its largest sister. Twenty-five mile long Dawes Glacier, at the head of Endicott Arm, averages approximately 175 feet above water level; its face spans a half-mile.

Sawyer Glacier calves house-sized chucks of ice.

### TIDEWATER GLACIERS, CALVING, AND ICEBERGS

Glaciers form on land as a result of the net accumulation of snow over hundreds, if not thousands of years. When the end – also called the face or terminus – of a glacier meets the ocean, we call that glacier a tidewater glacier. The end of a tidewater glacier is not very stable due to constant forward glacial flow. Glacier calving occurs when chunks of ice break off. These chunks of floating glacier ice are called icebergs. After the ice above the waterline calves, the ice below has nothing left to hold it in place and eventually will break off as well, shooting to the surface. These potentially dangerous bergs are thus called shooters.

The face of South Sawyer Glacier rises 200 feet above sea level and is approximately 900 feet deep below sea level. The largest icebergs usually calve under water. Most boat captains try to keep a minimum of a quarter-mile distance from the face of the glacier. They are not worried about calving ice falling on the boat, they are scared of shooters.

The Dawes Glacier calves and the spray almost reaches the top of Dawes' 200 feet terminus.

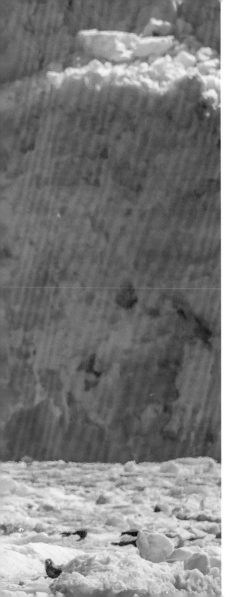

A boat passenger closely inspects a deep blue iceberg.

## *Growlers and bergy-bits*

A notable fact of both Sawyers and Dawes Glaciers is the relative abundance of deep-blue ice — formed under greater pressure and generally denser than the lighter shades. The glacier blue colors contribute to the spectacular array of free-floating ice of all sizes — from massive icebergs to low-lying "growlers", to the minor chunks dubbed "bergy-bits". Carved by the effects of sun and water, some resemble abstract sculpture as they jostle on the tide, gradually fading away. The greatest concentration of icebergs is near the glacial face, and this is especially true for South Sawyer. Larger bergs may survive long enough to reach the open waters of Stephens Passage, beyond Holkham Bay.

An immature bald eagle sits high on an iceberg, while harbor seals below seek refuge from predators on the pack ice.

### BLUE ICE

Glacier blue ice is a sight to behold and certainly a big reason to visit Tracy Arm-Fords Terror Wilderness.

Glacier blue ice is very dense. Fresh snowfall on a glacier contains about 80% air. After a year or so and under pressure from new snow above, the delicate snowflakes turn into tiny pellets called firn, which contains about 50% air. In Southeast Alaska, it does not take very long, maybe 4-6 years, for firn to turn into glacier ice with less than 20% air remaining between crystals. Over time and under increasing pressure, even more air will escape, making glacier ice heavy and dense. As light strikes this dense ice, the crystalline structure absorbs all colors of the light spectrum except blue. Glacier ice crystals refract blue light, and that is what our eye can see.

When ice calves off a glacier, the newly exposed ice appears exceptionally blue. The crystalline ice structure responsible for the blue color remains intact for only a few days. In time, air and surface melt breaks down the ice, causing it to fade to white — a color that denotes many tiny air bubbles in the ice.

## Wildlife in the arms

Of course, wildlife is a highlight of any visit. Seeing harbor seals is a virtual lock in Tracy Arm – dozens, sometimes hundreds, are visible on the ice floes near South Sawyer, which serve both as havens from shore predators (especially for young pups, who are born on the ice in late spring) and as sunning platforms, where the animals warm themselves and rest. A smaller, but significant number of seals utilize the ice near the face of Dawes Glacier. Mountain goats, too, are regularly spied by sharp-eyed viewers, often hundreds or thousands of feet up the fjords' sheer rock walls. During early season, April and sometimes May, goats may browse just above sea level, searching for the first tender shoots or even foraging for seaweed. Bears are present throughout the wilderness area, patrolling the intertidal zone, especially early and late in the day. Sea birds – including arctic terns, marbled murrelets and pigeon guillemots (easily identified by their red feet) – are common near the glaciers. Larger marine mammals, such as humpback whales, killer whales, Stellar sea lions and harbor porpoises, are rare inside either Tracy or Endicott Arms, but are commonly spied on the 45-mile journey between Stephens Passage and Juneau.

As far as the eye can see harbor seals are hauled out on the pack ice, to rest and give birth to their pups in massive numbers in May and June.

## Harbor seals

More than a 1,000 harbor seals use the icebergs close to the glacier fronts as haul-outs during the summer in Tracy Arm-Fords Terror Wilderness. The icebergs afford the seals protection from land predators such as wolves and their only marine predators, the killer whales. The most concentrated use of the ice is in front of the South Sawyer Glacier. Usually the harbor seals move onto the icebergs in the spring in order to have their babies (pups). Harbor seals are, of course, mammals; that is, they are hairy, warm-blooded, air-breathing animals that suckle their young. Pups weigh about 24 pounds at birth and adults weigh in around 180 pounds with males slightly larger than females.

Harbor seals can dive to depths exceeding 600 feet and can remain submerged for more than 20 minutes. Female average life expectancy is 32 years, while a typical male lives 26 years.

## Mountain goats

Mountain goats thrive along the steep rocky slopes of the Tracy Arm-Fords Terror Wilderness Area. This vertical environment provides unparalleled protection for the goats from their predators. In the summer the goats move into high alpine meadows 2,000 to 5,000 feet above the Arm's shoreline. During the winter goats move out of the high country, seeking escape from the deep snow. In the spring, visitors to the Arm can sometimes find goats at the tide line. Goats live for approximately 10 to 12 years. Males (billies) weigh in around 200 pounds and females (nannies) at around 160. Nannies usually give birth to a single baby (kid) in late May or early June. At

A mountain goat kid smells its mother or nanny.

birth a kid weighs approximately seven pounds and stands a foot high at the shoulders. Kids are precocious and can keep up with adults on the steep rocky terrain when only hours old.

A group of mountain goats forage in the seaweed at low tide just off the face of Sawyer Glacier.

47

## Black and brown bears

Black and coastal brown bears are most visible in the Tracy Arm-Fords Terror Wilderness during the early summer months of May and June. Just re-entering the world after a winter's hibernation, the bears forage along the tide line, and clamber up and down rocky slopes with surprising ease. Later in the season the bears leave the shoreline and move back up the river valleys (out of sight) to feed on plants, berries, and salmon that spawn in a few of the drainages.

Black bears (*Ursus americanus*) are the smallest of the North American bears. Adult bears stand about 30 inches at the shoulders and measure about 60 inches from nose to tail. Males outsize females, and an average adult weighs about 180 to 200 pounds. Brown bears (*Ursus arctos*) can be identified by their dished faces and prominent shoulder humps. Color isn't always a reliable guide—some black bears are brown, and some brown bears are almost black! Brown bears average double or more the size of the black bear; a huge male may reach 1,000 pounds, though such behemoths are rare.

At low tide, a black bear looks for food along the steep cliff-faced shoreline.

A coastal brown bear rests after feeding on the barnacles and mussels found at low tide on the steep cliff walls of the fjord.

# Bald eagles

The white heads of bald eagles dot the spruce trees along the route to Tracy Arm-Fords Terror. Often, the eagles will perch on icebergs. Found only in North America, Southeast Alaska's bald eagle population by itself is many times larger than in all the other states combined—an estimated 20,000 birds. The main diet of bald eagles is fish, and the abundant fish resources of Alaska including salmon and herring let these birds of prey thrive.

The United States' national symbol remains brown until sexual maturity between 4 and 5 years old when the eagle's head and tail feathers turn distinctively white. Bald eagles can live up to 30 years, but the average life spans 15 to 20 years. They grow about three feet tall, weigh 8 to 18 pounds, and may attain a seven-foot plus wingspan.

LEFT: A bald eagle takes flight from a blue iceberg.. ABOVE: Twenty-seven eagles perch on an iceberg at the entrance of Tracy Arm.

## Arctic terns

Arctic terns hold the record for the longest migration of any bird. Their approximate 25,000 mile round-trip migration takes them from Antarctica to Alaska. These lightweight birds (10 to 12 ounces) spend their summer in Tracy Arm, living around the edges at the face of the glaciers. These all-white birds have a distinctive black skull cap, red legs and a long, white, forked, swallow-like tail. They eat small fish, insects, krill and shrimp and live up to 30 years.

Glaucous-winged gulls perch on an iceberg.

## Ice birds

A variety of sea birds, including arctic terns, gulls, and kittiwakes, may be seen perching on icebergs and flying about near the active faces of all three Tracy Arm-Fords Terror glaciers. Though conditions in this world of ice, swirling tidal currents, and barren rock seem harsh, they provide ideal habitat—relative safety from predators, good nesting sites, and an abundant food supply. Each glacial calving creates a geyser that stuns clouds of shrimp-like krill and brings them to the surface. The birds aren't startled into flight by the thunderous commotion; they're answering the dinner bell.

A flock of birds fly around in front of Dawes Glacier in search of food.

A humpback whale raises its tail (flukes) for a dive while another exhales air through its twin blow holes, creating a distinctive plume of water vapor.

## Humpback whales

The passage from Juneau to Tracy Arm-Fords Terror can provide a good opportunity to see humpback whales. Humpbacks and killer whales typically do not enter the fjords themselves. Humpback whales usually congregate outside Holkham Bay in Stephens Passage, often in great numbers in August and September.

Humpbacks grow to lengths of 42 to 49 feet and weigh 25 to 40 tons with females being larger than males. Humpbacks are the sixth largest whale species in the world.

Humpbacks belong to a suborder of whales called baleen or toothless whales. Their throats are no wider than a grapefruit, and they savor dense clouds of zooplankton (mostly comprised of a shrimp-like crustacean called krill), and schools of herring-sized fish. They feed by taking a mouthful of prey-laden seawater, straining out the water, and gulping down what is left. The straining apparatus, known as baleen, hangs from the upper jaws in place of teeth and resembles rows of fine-toothed combs.

Humpbacks migrate, wintering in Hawaii or Mexico (where they give birth) and summering in Alaska, where the cold water combines with the long summer daylight to produce a sea rich in prey. Humpbacks feed almost constantly and consume over a third of a ton of food per day.

Water cascades off the flukes of a diving humpback whale. Researchers use the shape, size, patterns, markings and coloration of a humpback's tail to identify each individual animal.

A lone killer whale swims through the mirror calm waters reflecting the green of the spruce trees lining the shore.

Killer whales often travel in large groups called pods. These pods are usually large family groups that stay together for life.

## Killer whales

Killer whales are the wolves of the marine world. They usually hunt in packs, are the apex predators of the ocean, and cover a huge territory, sometimes thousands of square miles as their home range. A passenger is as likely to see a killer whale along the route to Tracy Arm as anywhere else in Southeast Alaska.

These toothed whales typically travel in family groups called pods. Killer whales average 23 to 33 feet and weigh 4 to 11 tons, depending on the sex of the animal; the males are larger. Familiar as the whale species featured at Sea World, the killer whales' distinctive black and white markings and shark-like fins make them easily recognizable in the wild. As track stars of the ocean world, these whales can reach speeds of approximately 34 miles per hour. Ancient whalers referred to them as "killer of whales" for their ability to kill much larger whales, though many of them prefer a fish diet and seldom or never eat marine mammals. Over time the name shortened to killer whale. Many people, in the interest of a kinder, gentler image, call them orcas.

59

Icy Falls, Tracy Arm.

## *A brush against the eternal*

In the end, a journey to Tracy Arm-Fords Terror Wilderness isn't about a checklist of creatures spotted, a collection of facts or figures, or an accounting of miles on a map. Surely such details add richness, but ultimate meaning lies in grasping the magnitude of what you've seen — the drama of creation and destruction that lies at the heart of all being, cast in a scale so grand it must be felt rather than understood. And fleeting images fill in the rest — skeins of mist draped across mountain shoulders, the sudden appearance of a seal's long-whiskered face at boatside, angled sunlight filtering through an iceberg. These are the small things that fuse into memory, reminding us we've brushed against the eternal.

From Juneau to Tracy Arm

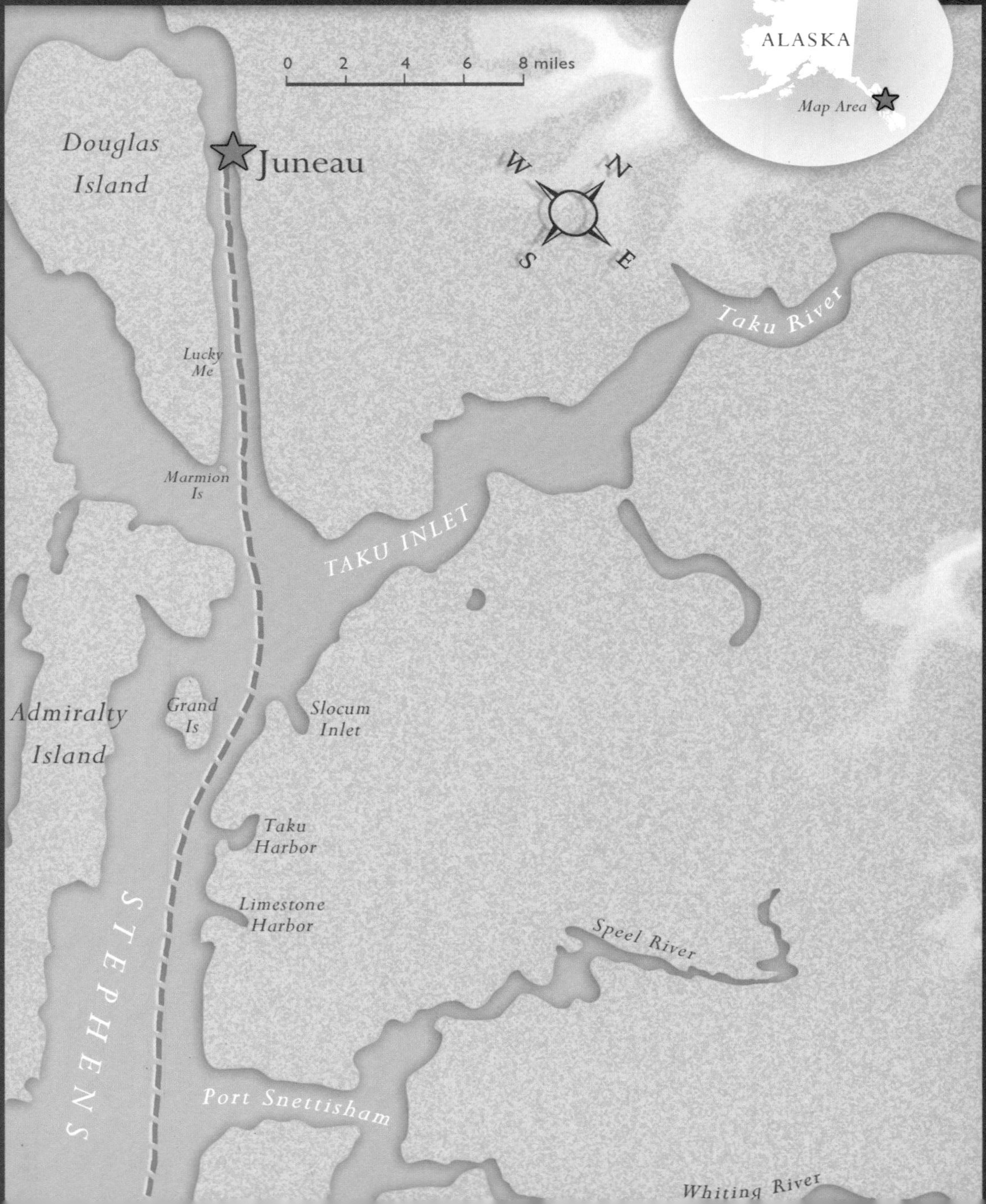

ALASKA

Map Area

N
W E
S

8 miles

0 2 4 6

Taku River

Whiting River

Speel River

TAKU INLET

Slocum Inlet

Taku Harbor

Limestone Harbor

Port Snettisham

Juneau

Lucky Me

Marmion Is

Grand Is

Douglas Island

Admiralty Island

STEPHENS